Presidential Elections

And Other Cool Facts

Presidential Elections

And Other Cool Facts

itten by **Syl Sobel**
istrated by Jill Wood

Barron's Educational Series, Inc.

To Izzy, who asked me to write this book.

All inquiries should be addressed to:
Barron's Educational Series, Inc.
250 Wireless Boulevard
Hauppauge, New York 11788
http://www.barronseduc.com

International Standard Book No. 0-7641-1438-7

Library of Congress Catalog Card No. 99-068666

Printed in Hong Kong
987654321

Contents

Who Will Lead the Country?

Maybe you've heard grown-ups talking about "the presidential election." Maybe you've heard someone say: "This is an election year." Or maybe the TV news has stories about people "running for president." Did you ever wonder what the presidential election is, and why adults spend so much time talking about it?

You probably know something about elections already. Your school may have a student government or a student council. When you and your classmates vote to put someone from your class in the

dent government, that is an election. When you and your friends ~~de~~cide whether to play baseball or play with sidewalk chalk, that's an ~~ele~~ction. An election is when people make choices by voting. ~~Wh~~ichever choice receives the most votes wins. A system in which ~~peo~~ple elect their leaders is called a *democracy*.

The United States is a ~~de~~mocracy. Elections are how ~~the~~ citizens choose who will ~~lea~~d the government. For ~~exa~~mple, the citizens of your ~~sta~~te elect the governor and ~~the~~ other leaders of your ~~sta~~te. And the citizens of ~~eac~~h state elect their ~~U.S~~. senators and ~~rep~~resentatives.

The senators and representatives make the country's laws in Congress. The leader, or chief executive, of the United States, is the president. The president's job is to make sure the government works properly and that the country's laws are enforced.

The president is also the commander of our army, navy, and air force. And when leaders of other countries need to meet with the leader of the United States, they meet with the president.

When the citizens elect the president of the United States, they are deciding who will lead the country. That is why the presidential election is so important.

The First Presidential Election Was No Contest

The first presidential election was in 1789. It wasn't really much of an election. George Washington was the only person running for president. He won. The same thing happened in 1792; no one ran against Washington.

Since then, there have been fifty-one presidential elections. In each one, two or more people have tried to be elected president of the United States.

The Rules for Electing the Preside

Every election has rules. The basic rules for electing the preside
are in the *U.S. Constitution*. The Constitution is the book of ru
that tells our government what its jobs are and how it is supposed to
do its work.

The Constitution has several rules about who can be president. They are as follows:

- The president must be at least 35 years old.
- The president must be born a citizen of the United States.

The Oldest and Youngest Elected Presidents

The oldest person who was elected president was Ronald Reagan. He was 73 years old when he was elected for the second time in 1984. John F. Kennedy was the youngest president ever elected. He was 43 years old when he was elected in 1960.

The Four-Term President!

Originally, the Constitution had no limit on the number of times a person could be elected president. Then, in 1951, the Constitution was changed, or amended, to add a rule that says a person can be elected to only two terms as president.

From the first presidential election in 1789 to the amendment in 1951, only one president was elected to more than two terms. That was Franklin Delano Roosevelt, who was elected president in 1932, 1936, 1940, and again in 1944!

- A person must have lived in the United States for fourteen years to be president.
- A person can be president for four years. That four-year period is called a *term*. The Constitution says a person can be elected to only two terms as president.

The Constitution also has rules about who can vote in an
_tion. U.S. citizens who are 18 years old or older may vote.

There are also special rules about how to decide who wins the
_sidential election. In most other elections, whoever gets the most
_es wins. But the Constitution creates a special system for electing
_ president called the *electoral college*.

OFFICES	PRESIDENT	VICE PRESIDENT	SENATE DISTRICT 2	CONGRESS DISTRICT 17	CONGRESS DISTRICT 5	COUNTY CLERK
DEMOCRATIC						
REPUBLICAN						
LIBERTARIAN						
REFORM						

The Electoral College

The electoral college involves two elections for president. In the first election, citizens vote for the person they want to be president. These votes are called the *popular vote*. But the person who gets the most popular votes does not automatically win the election.

Instead, people called *electors* will vote in a second election called the *electoral vote*.

Each person running for president, alled a *presidential candidate*, chooses people that they would like to be electors in each state. These people have promised to vote for their candidate in the electoral vote. The popular vote in each state determines which candidate's electors will vote in the electoral vote. In most states, whoever wins the popular votes in a state wins all of that state's electoral votes.

For example, let's look at a state that has fifteen electoral votes. Candidate Green and Candidate Brown are running for president. Candidate Brown wins the most popular votes in the state. Thus, the fifteen people on Candidate Brown's list become the state's electors and will vote for Brown in the electoral vote.

The number of electors a state has equals the number of its senators plus the number of its U.S. representatives. Every state has two senators. The number of U.S. representatives in a state depends on how many people live in the state. Every ten years the governme counts the number of people who live in the United States. This is called a *census*. If more people live in a state than in the last census the state may get more representatives. If fewer people live in the st than in the last census, or if the state has not gained as many people other states, it may get fewer representatives.

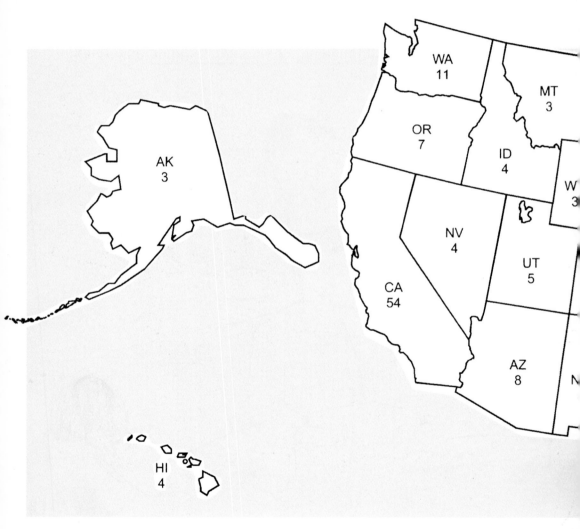

The states with the fewest people have only one U.S. resentative. So one U.S. representative plus two senators means y have three electoral votes. The Constitution also gives the District Columbia three electoral votes.

The state with the most electoral votes is California, with 54. w York is next with 33, and Texas has 32. After that are Florida (25), nsylvania (23), Illinois (22), and Ohio (21). The number of electoral es a state gets could change, depending upon the results of the sus every ten years.

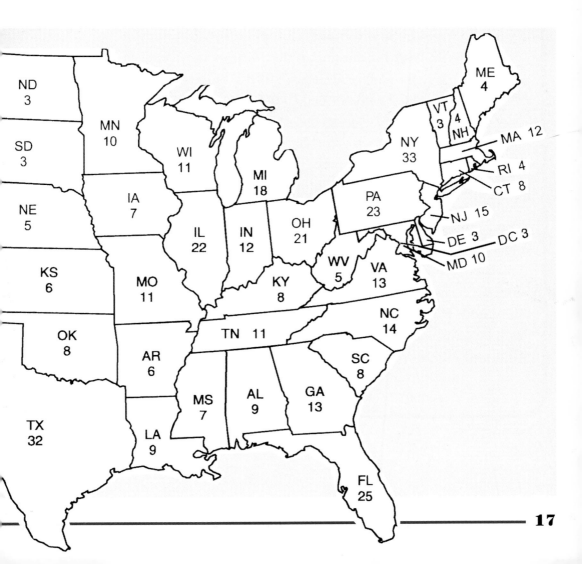

The Winners Who Lost!

Under the electoral college system, someone can win the most popular votes for president, but still lose. That has happened three times.

In 1824, four candidates ran for president. Andrew Jackson won the most popular votes. He also won the most electoral votes, but not enough for a majority. The Constitution says that, if no one wins a majority of the electoral votes, the House of Representatives must choose the president. The House elected John Quincy Adams to be president.

In 1876, Samuel J. Tilden won the popular vote. He also won the most electoral votes, but fell one elector short of the majority he needed to be president. Electoral votes in three states still needed to be counted. Both Tilden and Rutherford B. Hayes claimed they won the votes in those states. Congress picked a group of people called the Electoral Commission to decide who won those electoral votes. The commission decided that Hayes won those electoral votes, and he became president.

In 1888, more people voted for Grover S. Cleveland, who was president at the time, than for his opponent, Benjamin Harrison. However, the states Harrison won had 233 electors, while Cleveland had 188. So Harrison became the president.

After the popular election, the electors in
h state meet to vote for president. Their votes
 counted several weeks later in Congress.
ichever candidate gets a *majority*—more than
—of the electoral votes wins. Of course,
ryone knows before the electors vote which
didate will win. That's because everyone knows
hen which candidate's electors were chosen on
ction Day.

The electoral college is a complicated
tem. The important thing to remember is that
election day, when people vote for a candidate,
y are actually voting for their candidate's
ctors.

The Presidential Campaign

Elections for president are held every four years. Here's an easy way to remember which years are election years: Election years always end in numbers that can be divided by four. The years 2000, 2004, 2008, 2012, and so on, are all presidential election years. *Election Day* is the Tuesday after the first Monday in November.

NOVEMBER

Sunday	Monday	Tuesday	Wednesday	Thursday	Friday	Saturday
		1 ELECTION DAY	2	3	4	5
6	7	8	9	10	11 VETERAN'S DAY	12
13	14	15	16	17	18	19
20	21	22	23	24 THANKSGIVING	25	26
27	28	29	30	31		

People who want to be president begin
nning for the election very early, usually more
n one year before the election. The period of
e from when people first announce that they
nt to be president until Election Day is called
presidential campaign.

The first step in the campaign is when the
jor *political parties* choose their presidential
didates. Political parties are groups of people
o share many of the same ideas about how the
ernment should work. For most of its history,
country has had two major political parties.
parties have had different names. There have
n parties called the Whigs, the Federalists, and
Democratic-Republicans. The two major
ties now are the Democrats and the
ublicans.

There have also been many smaller political
ties. These are called *third parties.* Most
sidential elections have one or more third-party
didates. Most of the time, candidates for the
d parties get many fewer votes than the
didates for the Democrats and Republicans.

The campaign begins when people announce
they want to be the candidate for their party.
one who meets the constitutional requirements
be president. Usually, presidential candidates
leaders of the government, such as senators,
J.S. representatives, or governors of states.
eral candidates usually compete against each
er to become their party's candidate.

Voters in each state help to pick their party's candidate. Some states hold *primary elections* to help select the candidates for each party. These elections are held early in the election year, between February and June. In other states, members of the political parties get together in a meeting called a *caucus*. The primary elections and the caucuses have the same purpose. Voters decide which person they want to be their party's candidate in the presidential election in November.

The candidates spend much time and effort before the primary elections and caucuses trying to win votes. Candidates travel from state to state. They make speeches, meet people at parades, picnics, and ball games, and appear on television. Usually, there are many candidates running for president in the first primaries and caucuses. By the time the last primaries and caucuses are held, only a few candidates are left. The rest have quit the campaign because they have been getting very few votes. They know they do not have enough votes to become their party's candidate.

Then in the summer, after the caucuses and primary elections are over, each party has a big meeting called a *convention*. The Republicans have a convention, and the Democrats have a convention. Sometimes, third parties have conventions, too. At the conventions, representatives from each state, called *delegates*, vote to choose their party's candidate. The number of delegates voting for each candidate usually depends on the number of votes candidate got in the primary elections and caucuses. The more votes a candidate won in the primary elections and caucuses, the more delegates the candidate has at the convention. Sometimes the delegates vote several times until they pick a candidate.

Third-Party Candidates

The best finish by a third-party candidate was in 1912. Theodore Roosevelt of the Progressive Party came in second place. Roosevelt was a Republican president from 1901 to 1909. The president in 1912, William Howard Taft, was also a Republican. After the Republican's chose Taft to run for a second term in 1912, Roosevelt formed the Progressive Party. That party was also called the Bull Moose Party, because once, when someone asked Roosevelt how he felt, he said he felt "fit as a bull moose." Roosevelt got more popular votes and more electoral votes than Taft. But Woodrow Wilson, the Democratice Party candidate, won the popular vote and more than half the electoral votes, so he won the election.

Actually, the Republican Party started off as a third party. In the 1850s, The Whig Party was losing its popularity. A third party was taking its place. That was the Republican Party, led by Abraham Lincoln.

Conventions are very colorful, noisy events. They feature big bands, lots of balloons, and thousands of delegates, political party members, and their families. Some delegates and party members wear funny costumes, sing songs, and chant slogans, to show how much they love their party and their candidate. The leaders of the

ties give speeches, saying how much they
port their party and their candidate.
netimes, famous actors and sports stars give
eches, too. Finally, the candidates give
eches, saying what they would do if they
re elected president.

The main purpose of the convention is to pick the party's candidate. But the conventions are also a time for members of the party to celebrate— and to show off their candidate to the voters. People watch the conventions on television and read about them in the newspapers and magazines. The voters learn about the candidates by what they say, and by what people say about them, at the conventions. The party members show lots of support for their candidates at the conventions because they know voters are watching.

Keeping It in the Family

Three sets of relatives have been president, including one father and son. John Adams was the second president, elected in 1796. His son, John Quincy Adams, was elected the sixth president in 1824.

Benjamin Harrison, the twenty-third president elected in 1888, was the grandson of the ninth president, William Henry Harrison, who was elected i 1840. And Theodore Roosevelt and Franklin D. Roosevelt were cousins. Theodore Roosevelt became the twenty-sixth president in 1901. Franklin Roosevelt, the thirty-second president, was elected four times starting in 1932.

Franklin
Delano
Roosevelt

Theodore
Roosevelt

Benjamin
Harrison

John
Quincy
Adams

John Adams

William
Henry
Harrison

First Ladies

Neither the Constitution nor the laws of the United States give any jobs or responsibilities to the president's family. But many of the wives of the presidents have earned fame and admiration for work they did while their husbands were president.

Some of the presidents' wives became famous as hostesses. Dolley Madison, wife of the fourth president, James Madison, was particularly well known as the White House hostess. Indeed, even before her husband became president, she served as White House hostess for Thomas Jefferson, the third president, because Jefferson's wife had died before he became president.

Dolley Madison

Lou Hoover

Eleanor Roosevelt

Other presidents' wives have become famous for important work they did outside of the White House. Lou Hoover, wife of Herbert Hoover, was active in many organizations and served as president of the Girl Scouts of America. Eleanor Roosevelt, wife of Franklin D. Roosevelt, became known for supporting programs to help underprivileged people. Lady Bird Johnson, wife of Lyndon Johnson, was famous for making America beautiful. She helped to create parks in cities and improve the landscape along highways throughout the United States.

The president's wife has been called the "First Lady" since about 1877; that name was used to refer to Lucy Hayes, wife of Rutherford B. Hayes. So far, all of the presidents have been men. When a woman is elected president, what do you think the president's husband will be called?

Lady Bird Johnson

Lucy Hayes

Then the campaign enters its final months. The candidates travel around the country. Big crowds of people gather to hear the candidates speak. Often, the families of the candidates travel around the country, too. Sometimes they stand on stage with the candidate. Sometimes they make speeches saying why the candidate would be a great president.

The candidates usually hold several *debates*. At the debates, the candidates appear together, answering questions and explaining what they would do if they were president. These debates are usually on television, so voters around the country can watch and decide who to vote for.

Finally, November arrives and it's Election Day. Millions of citizens vote in every state, city, and town in the United States. The votes are counted. The person who gets the most votes in each state wins that state's electoral votes. Even though the electors don't vote until January, everyone knows in November who the winner is.

The news media, that is, the newspapers, radio, and television news, watch presidential elections very closely. They know that choosing a president is a very important event for the United States. They try to tell the people as much as they can about the candidates for president and vice president. This helps voters decide who to choose.

The Paper Got It Wrong

The news media also try to predict who will win. The experts who make these predictions are often right. But there is at least one well-known time when they were very wrong. In 1948, Harry S. Truman ran for a second term against Thomas Dewey. It was a close election. While the votes were still being counted, one newspaper, the *Chicago Tribune*, was so sure Dewey would win that it printed a front page story with the headline "Dewey Defeats Truman." When all of the votes were counted, however, Truman had won. There is a very famous picture of President Truman holding up the paper with the incorrect headline, with a big smile on his face.

DEWEY DEFEATS TRUMAN

The President Who Counts Twice

Forty-one people have served as president. But the United States has had forty-two presidents. How can that be? Grover S. Cleveland was elected the twenty-second president in 1884. Four years later, he lost the election to Benjamin Harrison, who became the twenty-third president. (Remember, that was the election in which Cleveland won more popular votes, but lost the electoral vote.) Then, in 1892, Cleveland ran against Harrison and beat him, becoming the twenty-fourth president. So Cleveland counts as one person, but as two presidents.

The person elected president does not take over right away. The new president needs time to select the people who will be advisors and help run the government. The new president begins the four-year term on the January 20th after the election. That day is called *Inauguration Day*.

What If Something Happens to the President?

What if the president gets in an accident or gets too sick to do the job of president more? What happens if the president dies? at if the president behaves very badly, and igress decides to remove the president from ce? (The Constitution says Congress can do t, but Congress has never actually removed the sident.)

The Constitution has rules for what to do in e something happens to the president. The stitution creates the job of *vice president*. The e president's main job is to be the president of U.S. Senate. But the Constitution also says that ie president dies, quits, is removed, or is unable lo the job of president, the vice president omes president.

The vice president is elected at the same time he president. Each political party chooses teone to run as vice president at the same vention at which it chooses a presidential didate. Usually, the candidate for president ks the vice president, and the delegates at the vention approve the choice.

A party's candidates for president and vice president are called the party's *ticket*. That means that they are listed together on the voting ballot. Citizens vote for a party's presidential candidate and vice presidential candidate together. An electoral vote for the presidential candidate also counts as an electoral vote for the vice presidential candidate.

The vice presidential candidates also travel
und the country making speeches. Sometimes
v travel and appear with their party's presidential
didate. Sometimes they campaign on their own.

A vice president who becomes president
st choose someone to be the new vice president.
Senate and the House of Representatives must
e to approve the new vice president. Once they
the new vice president will become president if
new president cannot continue. The new
ident and vice president will do their jobs until
next scheduled election.

And what if something happens to the
ident and vice president at the same time? This
never happened. But just in case, Congress has
e laws that give the order in which other
ers of the government would take the place of,
ucceed, the president. This *order of succession*
ns with the two leaders of Congress. They are
Speaker of the House of Representatives
wed by the President Pro Tempore of the
te. After that, the leaders of the government
cies that work for the president would
eed.

The Constitution and Congress have made
rules so that there is always a president to
the country, and that every four years the
ens can elect a president.

Order of Succession

1. Vice President

2. Speaker of the House

3. President Pro Tempore
   of the Senate

4. Secretary of State

5. Secretary of the Treasury

6. Secretary of Defense

7. Attorney General

8. Secretary of the Interior

9. Secretary of Agriculture

10. Secretary of Commerce

11. Secretary of Labor

12. Secretary of Health
    & Human Services

13. Secretary of Housing
    & Urban Development

14. Secretary of Transportation

15. Secretary of Energy

16. Secretary of Education

17. Secretary of Veterans' Affairs

The Vice President Becomes President

Nine times in this country's history, a vice president has become president. The first time this happened was in 1841, when John Tyler succeeded William Henry Harrison after Harrison died.

The other vice presidents who succeeded presidents were as follows:

Millard Fillmore, who became president in 1850 after Zachary Taylor died.

Andrew Johnson, who succeeded Abraham Lincoln after Lincoln was shot and killed in 1865.

Chester A. Arthur, who became president in 1881 after James A. Garfield was shot and killed.

Theodore Roosevelt, who succeeded William McKinley after he was shot and killed in 1901.

Calvin Coolidge, who became president in 1923 upon the death of Warren G. Harding.

Harry S. Truman, who in 1945 succeeded Franklin D. Roosevelt after his death.

Lyndon B. Johnson, who became president in 1963 after John F. Kennedy was shot and killed.

Gerald R. Ford, who in 1974 became president after Richard M. Nixon resigned.

Here is one more thing for you: a list of all of the people who have been president, the years in which they served, and the name of their political party.

The Presidents of the United States

PRESIDENT	YEARS	PARTY
1. George Washington	1789–1797	Federalist
2. John Adams	1797–1801	Federalist
3. Thomas Jefferson	1801–1809	Democratic-Republican
4. James Madison	1809–1817	Democratic-Republican
5. James Monroe	1817–1825	Democratic-Republican
6. John Quincy Adams	1825–1829	Democratic-Republican
7. Andrew Jackson	1829–1837	Democrat
8. Martin Van Buren	1837–1841	Democrat
9. William H. Harrison	1841	Whig
10. John Tyler	1841–1845	Whig
11. James K. Polk	1845–1849	Democrat
12. Zachary Taylor	1849–1850	Whig
13. Millard Fillmore	1850–1853	Whig
14. Franklin Pierce	1853–1857	Democrat
15. James Buchanan	1857–1861	Democrat
16. Abraham Lincoln	1861–1865	Republican
17. Andrew Johnson	1865–1869	Democrat*
18. Ulysses S. Grant	1869–1877	Republican
19. Rutherford B. Hayes	1877–1881	Republican
20. James A. Garfield	1881	Republican
21. Chester A. Arthur	1881–1885	Republican
22. Grover S. Cleveland	1885–1889	Democrat

23. Benjamin Harrison	1889–1893	Republican
24. Grover S. Cleveland	1893–1897	Democrat
25. William McKinley	1897–1901	Republican
26. Theodore Roosevelt	1901-1909	Republican
27. William H. Taft	1909–1913	Republican
28. Woodrow Wilson	1913–1921	Democrat
29. Warren G. Harding	1921–1923	Republican
30. Calvin Coolidge	1923–1929	Republican
31. Herbert C. Hoover	1929–1933	Republican
32. Franklin D. Roosevelt	1933–1945	Democrat
33. Harry S. Truman	1945–1953	Democrat
34. Dwight D. Eisenhower	1953–1961	Republican
35. John F. Kennedy	1961–1963	Democrat
36. Lyndon B. Johnson	1963–1969	Democrat
37. Richard M. Nixon	1969–1974	Republican
38. Gerald R. Ford	1974–1977	Republican
39. James E. Carter	1977–1981	Democrat
40. Ronald W. Reagan	1981–1989	Republican
41. George Bush	1989–1993	Republican
42. William J. Clinton	1993–present	Democrat

Andrew Johnson ran as Abraham Lincoln's vice presidential candidate in the election of 1864. Johnson was a Democrat and Lincoln was a Republican, but they ran together on the National Union party ticket. That party consisted of Democrats and Republicans who wanted to keep the country together during the Civil War. When Lincoln was killed in 1865, Johnson became president.

Conclusion

You have learned all about presidential elections. You have learned what the rules are to run for president, and what the rules are for electing a president. You have learned about the electoral college, which actually votes for the president. And you have learned that someone can be president for a four-year term, and can be elected for only two terms.

You have also learned about presidential campaigns. You have learned about groups of people called political parties, who share many ideas about what the government should do. The parties pick their presidential candidates using primary elections, caucuses, and conventions. And you have learned that every four years, on the Tuesday after the first Monday in November, citizens vote for president.

Along the way, you have also learned many other things about the presidents and presidential elections.

There is a saying in this country: Anyone can grow up to be president. Maybe, someday the president will be you!!

Presidential Birthplaces

Eight presidents have been born in Virginia, which is why it is sometimes called the "Mother of Presidents." The Virginia-born presidents are George Washington, Thomas Jefferson, James Madison, James Monroe, William Henry Harrison, John Tyler, Zachary Taylor, and Woodrow Wilson.

Ohio is the next most popular birthplace of presidents. It was home to seven. They are Ulysses S. Grant, Rutherford B. Hayes, James Garfield, Benjamin Harrison, William McKinley, William H. Taft, and Warren G. Harding. Massachusetts and New York each were the home states of four presidents. Massachusetts had John Adams, John Quincy Adams, John F. Kennedy, and George Bush. New York had Martin Van Buren, Millard Fillmore, Theodore Roosevelt, and Franklin D. Roosevelt.

Glossary

Caucus: A meeting that members of the political parties have in some states to help choose presidential candidates for their parties.

Census: Every ten years the government counts the number of people who live in the United States. The number of people who live in a state determines the number of electoral votes each state gets.

Convention: A big meeting at which members of the political parties from all across the country pick their presidential and vice presidential candidates. Each party has its own convention to pick its own candidates.

Debates: Meetings at which the presidential candidates appear together. They give speeches, answer questions, and explain what they would do if they were elected president.

Delegates: The members of the political parties who meet at their party's convention to pick their presidential and vice presidential candidates.

Democracy: A system of government in which people elect their leaders.

Election Day: The day when citizens all across the United States vote for president. Congress has made a law that says Election Day is the Tuesday after the first Monday in November.

ctoral College: The system for electing the president. Citizens ˈe for electors in each state, and the electors vote for president. ˈandidate who wins the most votes in a state wins all of the ˈe's electoral votes.

ctoral Votes: The votes that the presidential electors cast. The ˈtoral vote determines who will be president.

uguration Day: The day on which the newly elected president ˈins the four-year term. The Constitution sets Inauguration Day ˈanuary 20th in the year after the election.

jority: More than half of the total number of votes wins the ˈsidental election.

itical Parties: Groups of people who share many of the same ˈas about how the government should work.

ular Vote: The votes that citizens cast for candidates on ˈction Day. But the popular vote doesn't actually elect the ˈsident. The electoral vote does.

sidential Campaign: The period of time from when people ˈt announce that they want to be president until Election Day.

sidential Candidates: The people who are trying to be ˈted president.

mary Elections: Elections that some states hold to help select ˈsidential candidates for the political parties. These elections ˈheld early in the election year, between February and June.

ccession: If something happens to the president, the vice ˈsident takes the place of, or succeeds, the president. If ˈnething happens so that the vice president cannot do it, ˈngress has made laws that give the order in which other leaders ˈhe government would take the president's place. This is called ˈorder of succession.

Term: The amount of time that someone keeps a job to which he or she is elected. The Constitution says the term for the president is four years. The president can only be elected to two terms.

Third Parties: Because there have usually been two major political parties in the United States, smaller political parties are called third parties.

Ticket: The presidential and vice presidential candidates for a political party are listed together on the voting ballot. Citizens vote for a party's presidential candidate and vice presidential candidate together. An electoral vote for the presidential candidate also counts as an electoral vote for the vice presidential candidate.

U.S. Constitution: The book of rules that tells the U.S. government how it is supposed to do its work.

Vice President: The person who becomes president if the president dies, quits, is removed, or is unable to do the job of president. The vice president is elected at the same time as the president.

elected Bibliography

singame, Wyatt, *The Look-It-Up Book of Presidents* (Random House, NY,
), 159 pages.
An excellent biographical and historical sketch of each president and
presidential election from George Washington through Bill Clinton.

berg, Barbara Silberdick, *Electing the President* (Twenty-First Century Books,
1995), 61 pages.
For readers in middle grades, it discusses the presidential election process,
including primaries, nominations, national conventions, campaigns, and the
electoral college.

ler, Paula N. and Justin Segal, *The Presidents Almanac* (Lowell House,
Angeles, CA, 1996), 95 pages.
A comprehensive and entertaining book about presidents and the presidency.
A running timeline that accompanies biographical sketches of each president
describes important events in American history during each term of office. It
also contains many fun facts about the presidents, their first ladies, and
families.

Kathleen, *Lives of the Presidents—Fame, Shame (and What the Neighbors
ght)* (Harcourt Brace & Company, San Diego, CA, 1998), 95 pages.
Detailed biographical sketches of every president, with emphasis on their
habits and personalities as men, husbands, fathers, friends, and neighbors.

ps, Louis, *Ask Me Anything About the Presidents* (Avon Books, NY, 1994),
ages.
Written in a question and answer style, this book contains many odd and
nusual facts about the presidents. It also contains brief biographical
ketches of each president and tables with information about presidents,
ice presidents, and first ladies.

REFERENCES

Congressional Quarterly's Guide to U.S. Elections, Third Edition (Congressio
Quarterly, Washington, DC, 1994).
> A comprehensive reference on U.S. political parties and presidential electi
> plus coverage of elections for Congress and governor in each of the states
> For a more concentrated treatment of the information on presidential
> elections, see *Presidential Elections 1789–1996* (Congressional Quarterly
> Washington, DC, 1997).

Encarta96 Encyclopedia (Microsoft, Redmond, WA, 1996).
> CD-ROM encyclopedia provides overview of presidents and presidential
> elections.

The World Book Encyclopedia (World Book, Inc., Chicago, IL, 1999).
> Excellent biographical sections of each president, plus an overview sectio
> on presidential elections.

Scholastic Encyclopedia of the Presidents and Their Times, by David Rubel
(Scholastic, NY, 1994).
> A thorough account of each president, presidential campaign, and import
> events and prominent people that were making history during each
> presidency.

The Dorling Kindersley Visual Encyclopedia (Dorling Kindersley Limited,
London, 1995).
> This children's encyclopedia includes a table listing the presidents of the
> United States.